The Plane Ride

PETER SLOAN &
SHERYL SLOAN

First the plane is towed
out of the hangar.

Next the plane's tanks
are filled with fuel.

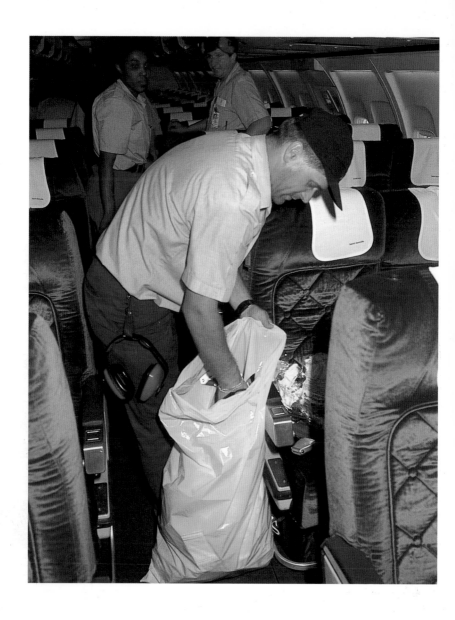

Then the cleaners clean
the plane.

After this the pilot and
the crew get on the
plane.

Next the baggage is put
on the plane.

Then the passengers get on the plane.

Finally the plane flies into the sky.
When it lands, the passengers will be a long way from home.